12 LAWS

OF KARMA

MANHARDEEP SINGH

CONTENTS

INTRODUCTION

In Sanskrit, Karma literally means "action". According to experts, there are often misunderstandings about what Karma really is and how it applies to our lives. This book will help shed light on what Karma is, the philosophy behind it, and its basic principles, known as the 12 Laws of Karma.

Most people have a basic concept of Karma. For example, you may have heard the phrase "what goes around comes around". Maybe you have the intuition that we get what we deserve in life. But what are The Laws of Karma? And what should you do to make sure you don't attract bad Karma?

If you look at Karma as "what goes around comes around," you are missing out. In fact, the 12 Laws of Karma are the guidelines for a better life.

Once you know how each of the 12 Laws of Karma work, you can learn to live in a way that creates good Karma in all areas of your life. It can help you in everything from your relationship to your career, your financial situation and your self-confidence.

Whether you want to generate more positive energy or get rid of bad Karma (or curses), this book gives you a better sense of how to improve your Karmic position.

What exactly is Karma?

The definition of Karma may change depending on who you ask. Some stick to the traditional meaning of the Eastern religions, while others interpret it from a more Western perspective of good and bad. As a result, it can lead to different views on how Karma applies to life.

For example, the Berkley Center for Religion, Peace and World Affairs at Georgetown University says that Karma is the Hindu view of causality in which good thoughts, actions, and words can produce beneficial effects, while bad thoughts, actions, and words can lead to harmful effects.

However, many experts like to see Karma as more than just "good" or "bad."

According to Dr. Jennifer Rhodes, a licensed psychologist, Karmas are the situations or interactions that help us achieve our ultimate purpose.

**We get distracted and miss messages
which make us believe we have a lot
of 'bad' Karma. But those situations
are simply signs for us to course-
correct and move forward toward
our higher purpose.**

The journey of life is not about perfection, but about destroying what we are not and becoming what we really are. Tejal Patel, a specialist in meditation and mindfulness, sees Karma as a cycle of cause and effect related to action rather than the result.

**Karma is a philosophy of how to live
our lives so we can truly become the
best version of ourselves and live the
most fulfilling life we desire.**

And since it does not set the future in stone, says Patel, we can change our life through our current decisions, thoughts and actions.

Karma is a law of nature. Karma is the currency of your life. With Karmic actions, you can buy and create all of your life experiences - good and bad, pleasant and unpleasant. Karma is The Law of Cause and Effect, according to which every person determines his own fate with his thoughts, words and actions.

Basically, if you push something, it moves. Now expand this idea and realize that we make the entire universe up with movements and reactions to movements.

Your body gets created by the lovemaking movements of your parents, then by the movement of the sperm into the egg, the reproduction of the zygote, the formation of organs, and the absorption of nutrients. Our body keeps itself alive through movements: visible movements, invisible movements and millions of tiny electrochemical movements.

The entire universe comprises spins - from galaxies to societies, to electrons that revolve around the nucleus of an atom. Movement is the essence and quality of all creation. So what keeps everything going?

You can say that the universe works on the fuel of Karma. As Newton's Law of Action says, every action has an equal and opposite reaction. This is how Karma works.

A good way to understand the complexities of Karmic law is to observe how Karmas manifest in and around you. Life is a living textbook on the Laws of Karma. You can observe how life so often creates exactly what you want or fear most. Notice how the most vehement persecutors in any situation inevitably seem to become the persecuted. See how your own good deeds can rejoice your heart and create an opening for more goodness to come into your life.

Even movie scripts and novels reflect an intuitive understanding of these laws, as good defeats evil almost always, even if only moments before the final credit roll!

You already know the Laws of Karma

Basically, Karma is a law of the universe like any other, but society has not understood it fully yet. So sometimes it's used as a joke, like in "ha ha, that must have been your Karma!" This line would be like making a joke after someone falls, saying "ha ha, that must have been gravity!" Well?

Humans have been using the Laws of Karma since the beginning, when an unknown caveman first discovered that putting his hand in the fire created pain and did not do so again.

Karma is like the wind

By visualizing the idea of Karma, you can imagine a large and deep lake - the lake of your soul. When the lake is still, you can see its depths full of life. But on a windy day, with leaves and twigs hitting the surface of the water, it gets covered in ripples where the view of its depths becomes obscured.

In this metaphor, you can find examples of two types of Karma:

Fresh Karmas: The wind is analogous to the current winds of Karma that are recently being whipped up by your own endless thoughts, words and actions.

Old Karmas: Twigs and leaves on the surface of the water would be analogous to old solidified Karmas that are not so easily discarded, such as Karmas related to your family or cultural traditions. You are more or less stuck with these Karmas.

Now, here's the deal. You may not have much control over all those leaves and old Karmas, but you have the option to choose how the winds of the Karmas that you are creating right now will blow.

Even if you have a lot of old Karmic debris in the lake of your soul, if the current winds remain calm, the Karmic disorder moves towards the perimeter of the lake, leaving the depths visible through the clear surface of the lake. However, if you generate a lot of violent winds by performing all kinds of noisy, ego-based actions, you will have a messy and obstructive surface.

With many current Karmic winds, even if you only have a small amount of old debris from past actions, the surface of your lake will still get obscured by whatever is there, and also by the ripples created in the lake directly by the fresh Karmic winds.

The winds of new Karmas become still when you enter a state of inner peace. You can find inner peace by allowing your thoughts and actions to flow through you, unsullied by selfish desires or ego-based motives. When your surface waters are clear, you see more clearly what is really at the core of your being — the glorious light of your spiritual soul.

Now as a man is like this or like that,
according as he acts and according as he

behaves, so will he be;

a man of good acts will become good, a man of bad acts, bad;

he becomes pure by pure deeds, bad by bad deeds;

And here they say that a person consists of desires,

and as is his desire, so is his will;

and as is his will, so is his deed;

and whatever deed he does, that he will reap.

— Brihadaranyaka Upanishad

Karma, therefore, describes the concept of getting back from the universe whatever you offer, good or bad. By definition, it is fundamental for Hinduism and Buddhism to determine the next existence of a person based on the ethical network of the current one. But no matter what belief system you follow (or not), the concept of Karma can influence your life. That's because there are 12 Laws of Karma constantly in play, whether you realize it or not.

When you live by the 12 Laws of Karma, you create good Karma in your life, theoretically increasing the likelihood of good things to happen.

Everything we do creates corresponding energy that comes back to us in one form or another. Difficult Karmic experiences catalyze learning and growth, and can then lead to good Karma if we work towards positive change.

It would not be wrong to say that everything we do adds to our Karma:

- How we treat others;

- How we see our own role in the world;

- The way we use resources;

- How we develop our characters.

There are many perspectives on this matter; first, I would like to explain to you what Karma is not. Often misrepresented in the media, Karma has nothing to do with fate, universal justice or punishment.

Above all, I believe it is misleading to say that Karma has something to do with destiny because it is the opposite. People who believe in destiny think that they have a fixed future which is inevitable, while people who believe in Karma have their future in their hands and are fully responsible for their actions.

Therefore, Karma is, depending on how you interpret it, a concept that is based on the principle of cause and effect and has 12 rules. Simply put, every action, whether done by yourself or by others around you, has consequences. These can revert to you directly or indirectly.

Karma is more like a set of ethical rules, indicative, and works as a guide to morality and ethics. Viewing and using Karma in this context can have a positive impact on your life and personal development.

What is Bad Karma?

Bad Karma is a common term that is well established in everyday language. Colloquially, bad Karma means that when you do something wrong with someone, something bad happens to you. For example, you laughed because your friend's phone fell out of his hand, but then you dropped your phone yourself.

In the spiritual sense, Karma is the energy that comes from your thoughts and actions, which can be good or bad. Simply put, if your mind and behavior are bad, you will produce bad Karma, and if your behavior is good, you will produce good Karma.

However, if you consider Karma as a set of rules, there is no bad Karma in this colloquialism. We often confuse colloquial Karma with the first Karmic law, The Law of Cause and Effect.

The colloquial term has established itself because people have always wanted justice, especially when they feel unfairly treated. However, the danger of such a way of thinking is a lack of objectivity. People are subjective creatures and they quickly become emotional.

They often present Karma as the judge that restores balance in life.

If we look back at our example with phones, the friend you laughed at will cast your "bad Karma" as judge and think your phone fell out of your hand because you laughed at him before. In his opinion, Karma has restored "balance" by punishing you for laughing at him.

In the same context, difficult Karmic experiences catalyze learning and growth. Later, this can lead to good Karma if we work towards positive change.

What are the 12 Laws of Karma?

Everything is energy, including your thoughts and emotions, which are energy in motion. So everything you do creates corresponding energy that comes back to you in some form. In simpler words, everything you do generates a positive or negative consequence.

You can think of the Laws of Karma as guidelines to follow as you go about your daily life. The 12 Laws of Karma can help you understand how Karma really works and how to create good Karma in your life.

As we explore the 12 different Laws of Karma, think about how you have previously seen these laws come into play in your own life.

Also, consider how you can use your knowledge of these laws to create good Karma to support your dreams and goals. The key to moving beyond seemingly "bad" Karma is to live in a way that shows you are learning from the mistakes of the past.

As already mentioned, Karma has 12 laws. These are not laws in the genuine sense of the word, but guidelines and therefore should not taken as that. Here is a list of the 12 Laws of Karma.

1. The Law of Cause and Effect
2. The Law of Creation
3. The Law of Humility
4. The Law of Growth

5. The Law of Responsibility

6. The Law of Connection

7. The Law of Focus

8. The Law of Giving and Hospitality

9. The Law of Here and Now

10. The Law of Change

11. The Law of Patience and Reward

12. The Law of Significance and Inspiration

1

The Law of Cause and Effect

Whatever We Put Into the Universe Will Come Back to Us

When most people speak of Karma, they are probably referring to the great Law of Cause and Effect. According to this law, whatever thought or energy you put in, you will get it back, good or bad. To get what you want, you need to embody and be worthy of those things. It is the concept of you reap what you sow. For example, if you want love in your life, be loving to yourself. If you plant love and kindness, you shall get that in return.

The message here is like that of The Law of Attraction. Everything you give is also what you will receive, be it positive or negative. So if you want love in your life, be loving. If you want to enjoy financial abundance, be generous. And if you want to have honest and open relationships, you also need to offer authenticity and honesty to the people you care about.

The law encourages us that to get the things we want, we must also embody those things.

When you think everything is someone else's fault, you will suffer a lot. When you realize everything springs only from yourself, you will learn both peace and joy.
- Dalai Lama

Simply put, this law says that your thoughts and actions will have consequences. What these consequences look like and when they will take effect depends on the actions themselves. Good actions will have good consequences and bad actions, bad consequences.

Here's an example: if you are friendly and accommodating to people around you, you will make friends in return. It is like The Law of Attraction that says: like attracts like.

So, if you want to achieve peace, harmony and prosperity, you must act accordingly and do good.

In simpler words, what you give is also what you will receive. If you want love in your life, love your fellow men. If you want to have honest and open friends, get to know them honestly and with openness.

Key takeaway – Want happiness, give happiness.

2

THE LAW OF CREATION

LIFE DOES NOT HAPPEN BY ITSELF, WE NEED TO MAKE IT HAPPEN

The Law of Creation underscores the importance of life not simply happening to us. For things to happen in your life, you must act rather than wait for something to come your way automatically.

You are the co-creator of making what you want based on your intentions.

Ask yourself what you need to free up in order to create space for what you want to appear. Also, consider how you can use your skills, talents and strengths to create something that benefits not only yourself, but others as well.

The Law of Creation is about, you guessed it, creating. You don't wait for good things to happen in your life; you go out and make things happen. Oprahs and Beyoncés of the world are some of the prime examples of people who embody this Karmic law. They have used their talents, gifts and abilities to bless the world. They are constantly creating something, not only for the benefit of themselves but also for the benefit of others. So the power to create ideally is within you.

Life requires our participation to happen. It does not happen by itself. We are one with the Universe, both

inside and out.
Whatever surrounds us gives us
clues to our inner state.
Surround yourself with what you
want to have in your life and be
yourself.

According to the Karmic Law of Creation, we must be active participants in our lives if we want to get what we want. We can't just wait for things to happen to us. We must aim to surround ourselves with what we want in our lives, and look in our environment for clues about what we need. An important part of understanding The Law of Creation is seeing that things outside of us tell us what is happening within us. So if you don't like how your life looks right now, look inward and ask yourself what you need to change.

The Law of Creation also overlaps with The Law of Attraction. It says that you should actively invest time and effort in the things you want. You can't go through life expecting everything to come by itself.

**Work actively towards your goals
and create an environment in which
you feel comfortable.**

The environment is important in this context, as it has a significant influence on you and your well-being. It becomes part of you and influences you on many things. That is why it is your responsibility to act and adjust the environment according to your wishes.

If you are not happy with the way things are going in your life right now, look at your surroundings, decide what needs to be changed, and then change it.

**You cannot simply wait for things to
happen to you.**

An important part of understanding this law is seeing things outside of ourselves. These external things teach us what happens within us. If life doesn't look the way you want it, look inward. Ask yourself what needs to change. Ask yourself what you need to release.

Create space for things you desire to show up. Don't wait for great things to fall into your lap.

If chaos surrounds you, then there is an internal chaos that you must address. Surround yourself with what and who you want to be. Then you can create the future you want. Also, consider how you are using your skills, talents and strengths. Are you creating something that only benefits you? Or are you also benefiting others through your actions?

Key takeaway – Take efforts to create.

3

THE LAW OF HUMILITY

ONE MUST ACCEPT SOMETHING IN ORDER TO CHANGE IT

According to Paul Harrison, creator of The Daily Meditation, The Law of Humility works on the principle that you must be humble enough to accept that the present reality results from past actions. For example, if you blame your colleagues for poor performance at work, Harrison says, accept that you created this reality by not performing well.

To change something in your life, you first have to accept what is present. This is the premise of The Law of Humility. This is a characteristic that embodies many very successful people.

They are strong, kind, generous, and very humble people. But when they all started on their paths, they had to accept certain things about themselves and society.

So, no matter where you start, you need to know that if you can own your story and its facets that you have no control over, you can also own the path that follows. A happy, healthy, and successful future is yours for the taking.

So the first step is to accept something to change it. If all one sees is an enemy or a negative personality trait, then they cannot focus on a higher level of being.

Even in Buddhism, we can see the emphasis on the importance of The Law of Humility, as that you need to accept the true reality of something before you'll ever be able to change it.

If you constantly blame others for what you create or see someone who disagrees with you as a villain, you are out of step with reality. Therefore, it is very difficult to make the required changes. Consistent introspection helps you get the most out of The Law of Humility.

The Law of Humility says you have to accept things before you can change them.

You need to think humbly so that you can understand and accept your mistakes and weaknesses before taking the next step. You can change your direction only when you are ready to deal with the nasty truths about your actions.

Denying your own mistakes leads to you not working on them, and as a result, you do not improve your skills. If you are in this category, it's difficult to make the required changes.

**Consistent self-reflection helps you
make the most out of this law.**

Start where you are. If you want to change something, you really need to understand what to start with. Humbly accept your reality. Then work proactively to change what needs to be changed. Think about where you are in your life. Then work humbly on what you want.

Key takeaway – Accept reality, bring changes.

4

—·—

THE LAW OF GROWTH

WHEN WE CHANGE OURSELVES, OUR LIVES CHANGE TOO

Growth begins in us. To make the world a better place, start with yourself. Because actual change or personal development starts with what you can control, which is yourself, not someone else. The Law of Growth also looks at things that are beyond your control and how you accept those. Finally, you need to focus on yourself, not trying to control the people or things around you.

As the name suggests, The Law of Growth is about expansion within us. As we grow, change, and transform internally, our external reality will change and grow accordingly. This is where self-improvement and reading self-help and spiritual books come into play. And growth has no end. There is always something new to learn, shift, and heal.

Wherever you go, there you are. To grow spiritually, we need to change, not the people, place or things around us. All we have is ourselves. It's the only thing we can control. When we change who and what we have in our hearts, our lives change accordingly.

Wherever you go, there you are.

The message is that you need to change yourself before you expect it from the world around you. So how you use this control determines how the world responds to you. Therefore, focus on your own success before trying to control or change others. Let them figure out for themselves how things will change.

This law is all about personal growth and how you can achieve it. Because every change begins with you, the key to growth is in your hands.

The Law of Growth says that you have to change yourself to change the things around you.

There are things you can change and there are things you have to accept. After all, you can only control yourself completely.

You only have control over yourself.

As you grow and change, life will follow. Maybe even the world will follow.

Growth starts within us.

Key takeaway – Be the change you want to see in the world.

5

THE LAW OF RESPONSIBILITY

WE MUST TAKE RESPONSIBILITY FOR WHAT IS IN OUR LIVES

The Law of Responsibility is a reminder that you are the owner of what happens to you in life. This is a great reminder that what is happening to you is happening because of you. This eliminates the possibility of going outside to find the root of your problems.

You are the product of the choices you make.

The Law of Responsibility is about taking responsibility for everything that happens in our life, including the less good things. We handle the way we live our lives - not someone else. We handle how we appear in the world, how we allow others to treat us, and how we treat others. To enforce this law, you must take responsibility for the role you play in any situation.

If there is a problem in a person's life, then there is a problem in them. We reflect what surrounds us and what surrounds us reflects us. This is a universal truth. You have to take responsibility for what is in your life.

Like The Law of Growth, The Law of Responsibility aims to teach you to take ownership of the good and bad things you create, rather than keep looking outside to find excuses. The people and the surrounding environment are your choices and your decision.

If something does not suit you, it is your responsibility to change it.

Take responsibility for the things you created.

In this context, life's mistakes are just as important as the successes you benefit from. In fact, you learn the most from your mistakes.

You are the product of the choices you make. You take ownership of what's happening.

Don't make excuses. Deal with the bag. You may not have control over everything that happens to you. But you can take responsibility for your response to those things.

Key takeaway – Take ownership of your actions.

6

THE LAW OF CONNECTION

THE PAST, PRESENT AND FUTURE ARE ALL CONNECTED

The Law of Connection is based on the principle that everything in your life, including past, present and future, is interconnected.

Who you are today results from your previous actions.

And who you are tomorrow will result from your actions today.

The Law of Connection says that everything and everyone is connected in some way or the other. For example, even though your past, present, and future may seem completely different, they are still you. Everything you have experienced has led to the next thing, and the next thing, and the next thing. They all fit together. In the same fashion, we connect to others, too.

We help ourselves become learned, loved, honored, and respected. We do the same for others. There is always a connection. We just need to be observant and tune into it.

Also, perform the smallest and the least important tasks as well, because everything in the universe is connected. Each step adds to the progress. After all, someone has to do the initial work to get the job done. Neither the first nor the last step is more important. Both are must for the completion of the task. The past, the present and the future are all connected.

If you are wondering how to remove the vicious circle of bad Karma of past life experiences, The Law of Connection can help you with this. This law emphasizes the relationship between past, present and future and reminds us that our control over the present and the future helps us to get rid of the bad Karma of the past (whether from our current life or a previous life).

Another point mentioned by The Law of Connection is that it takes time to correct bad Karmas from the past. But every little step can have unexpectedly powerful effects. Therefore, all your actions, no matter how unimportant, affect you and your surroundings. Simply put, you need to take care of the little things too, so that other things come into your life. You need to remember that all tasks, first, middle or last, are important to achieve your goals.

Who you are today results from your previous actions. And who you will tomorrow be will result from your actions today.

We are all interdependent. Everything you have experienced before makes you who you are today. And that affects who you are tomorrow. This includes what you did and the people you interacted with. Our interaction with others also affects their lives.

Key takeaway – Present Karma heals previous Karma.

7

THE LAW OF FOCUS

WE CANNOT THINK OF TWO DIFFERENT THINGS AT A SAME TIME

Focusing on too many things at once can slow down the progress and lead to frustration and disappointment. So The Law of Focus encourages you to focus on one thing at a time.

If you focus on higher values like love and peace, then you're less likely to be distracted by heavy

feelings of resentment, greed or anger.

Although some of us may claim to be pro-multitaskers, but this inclination to do everything at once slows us down. The Law of Focus says you cannot invest your energy in two things at the same time. When you focus on one thing, you get more accomplished and get better results.

You cannot think of two things at once. If we focus on spiritual values, we will not have lower thoughts, such as greed or anger.

Our brain cannot follow multiple trains of thought with equal competency. So, if you have many important goals, try to act on them in a linear, ranked order rather than giving each goal only a part of your energy.

You can only focus on one thing at a time. This is important because the divided mind is more susceptible to negative thoughts and, therefore, more vulnerable to negative energies.

Mindfulness and meditation are great tools for improving focus.

Karma does not say you can't or don't have to multitask. Instead, it suggests that you will only know your full potential if you are focused. As mentioned at the start of the book, this is more of a guideline than hard rules you have to follow.

Direct your full attention to one task in order to accomplish it in the best possible way.

If you can follow the most important goal and eliminate everything else, you will have a better life. Your mind cannot provide equal energy to several things together.

If you have multiple goals to accomplish, try to work them through one step at a time. You can do this, for example, by doing the first step for 30 minutes and then the next step for next 30 minutes and so on. Use this approach for your work, your goals and your thoughts.

Key takeaway – Focus towards your single goal.

8

THE LAW OF GIVING AND HOSPITALITY

OUR BEHAVIOR SHOULD MATCH OUR THOUGHTS AND ACTIONS

Give what you believe in. This law will help you understand the value of your actions, reflecting on your deepest beliefs. For example, if you want to live in a peaceful world, you need to focus on creating peace for others.

This law speaks of selflessness, being giving to others, and obedience to what you preach. It is not just about talking and thinking good thoughts, but about walking, talking and acting based on these beliefs through action. For example, you believe in charitable donations. Thus, The Law of Giving and Hospitality states that when you get the opportunity to donate, you pursue and actually donate, instead of simply supporting it.

If a person believes that something is true, he will be called to show this truth sometime in his life. This is where one shows what they claim to have learned in practice. The focus here is on the relationship between belief and action. It guides and encourages the value of your actions that reflect your deepest beliefs.

This law also says that the universe will "test" you. Life gives us the opportunity to practice lessons and show you when you need to work hard on certain aspects of your character.

Your behavior should represent your thinking. Therefore, give and share out of inner conviction and not because of external factors.

This law also helps you in finding the inner motivation in your actions. The inner motivation means the motivation that comes from within, not from external elements. For example, if you donate money, it is because you want to help people, not because you want to receive praise from others.

Finally, it helps you understand the value of your actions. The meaning of the law is similar to "talk the talk and walk the walk."

Key takeaway – Be selfless and give others.

9

THE LAW OF HERE AND NOW

WE CANNOT BE PRESENT IF WE ARE LOOKING BACKWARD

To have peace of mind, you must embrace the present. This can only happen if you let go of negative thoughts or behaviors from your past. If you focus on past events, you will continue to relive them. One practice to be here and now is to get rooted in your senses.

**Look around the room you are in,
focus your eyes on something, blink,
and say 'I am here'.**

As you may guess, The Law of Here and Now is all about being present to the moment you have now. Right at this moment, holding this book. Most of us live life thinking about our past actions and what went wrong, replaying the same old recording over and over in our minds. If we live in here and now, and tap into the present with what we are doing, seeing, tasting, smelling, and feeling, we would not be so disconnected while talking to others, eating food, watching a movie, or spending alone time with ourselves. You realize that energy is different, and the experience is more rewarding and fulfilling.

Also, you cannot be here and now if you look back on what was, or worry about the future. Old ideas, old behavior patterns and old dreams prevent us from getting new ones.

In Buddhism, Karma is associated with the idea of accepting one's reality. Similarly, Buddhists often associate Karma with the concept of living in the present moment. If you are deeply drawn to the feelings, experiences and beliefs of the past, you will always have a foot in the past. Similarly, if you focus on anxiety or greed, you will always have one foot in the future. But in either way, you will never be here and now, in the present.

Following The Law of Here and Now means reminding yourself that the present is all you really have and it is the only place to engage and enjoy.

When you focus on the present, you will be able to decide which path you want to take. Although The Law of Connection states that the past is connected to the present and the future, it is not recommended to look at the past and plan for the future. Old habits prevent you from creating new habits and regularities.

You can't be in present when you look back.

Applying this rule will also help you reduce stress. To have peace of mind, you must embrace the present. This can only happen if you let go of negative thoughts or behaviors from the past.

Key takeaways – Live in the present moment.

10

—·—

THE LAW OF CHANGE

HISTORY REPEATS ITSELF UNTIL WE LEARN FROM IT AND CHANGE OUR PATH

Under this law, history will repeat itself until you learn the lesson and take steps to do something else to prevent this cycle.

Change gives you a new way to create a new future and a better version of yourself, free from the patterns of the past.

If you experience the same situation repeatedly (for example, you may be involved with the same unwanted partner), this is The Law of Change in action. This is a way for the universe to nudge you to learn a lesson.

The pattern will repeat if you do not learn from experience and do something else to become a better version and stop this vicious circle. The problem is that many people think too much and do not feel well enough.

To change the pattern and the problem, we must be able to connect thoughts and feelings and then adjust and make changes accordingly.

Meanwhile, if everything around you changes suddenly and dramatically, take it as a sign that you have made significant progress in your recent development.

The definition of madness is: "to do the same thing over and over again and expect different results." This statement fits the meaning of the tenth Karmic Law pretty well. It says:

The past repeats itself until you learn from it and take a new direction.

If you are not happy with your past, you need to learn from it to find a new way. Only then can you create a better future for yourself. Without the changes, nothing will change.

Change gives you a fresh path so that you can create a new future. And with that, you create a better version of yourself.

Free yourself from the patterns of your past.

Key takeaway – Learn to change your actions.

11

THE LAW OF PATIENCE AND REWARD

THE MOST VALUABLE REWARDS REQUIRE PERSISTENCE

To change the situation in the future, we must be consistent with our actions today.

It's no good living healthily for one day and then sabotaging it in the next.

This Karmic rule means "hard work pays off". Consistent work, to be precise. Even if you don't see the progress because of your actions, get there and work on it and don't give up on your big goals. Achieving great things takes time and patience, and it is better to live by the laws of this Karma, to not give up, rejoice in yourself, and love the little things you do during your journey.

Be consistent in your goals, and they will come to fruition.

Every reward requires effort first. Rewards of lasting value require persistence and patience. The real joy comes from doing what you have taken up to do and knowing the reward will arrive on time.

Simply put, The Law of Patience and the Reward claims that patience is prerequisite, regardless of what your goals in life are.

If you want immediate results, you will be disappointed. Your success will not be worth comparing with what you can accomplish.

Instead, find out what your real purpose is. Pursue this purpose and enjoy the reward of knowing that you are doing what you need to do in your current life. At the same time, the associated success (emotional and material) will follow.

The Law of Patience and Reward states that any reward requires work and patience.

Applying this principle to everyday life gives hope. Imagine that you have two goals. One is long and lasts several months, the other is short. Let's say your long-term goal is to get a raise and your short-term goal is to read 50 pages per week.

Let's say you have achieved both goals. The happiness you feel about getting a raise is more than the happiness you feel about achieving your short-term goal. This only makes sense, as you have worked harder and longer for the raise.

The more you sacrifice, the happier you become.

The reward feels greater because you spent more time and effort on it.

Simply put, this Karmic law says:

Long-term rewards require patience and constant work.

It may take longer than you planned, but finding joy in the work will make the reward even sweeter.

Key takeaway – Be patient and persistent.

12

THE LAW OF SIGNIFICANCE AND INSPIRATION

REWARDS RESULT FROM THE ENERGY AND EFFORT WE PUT INTO IT

We all play a role and have something to contribute to this world. What we share, at times, may seem small, but it can make a big difference in the lives of others.

The Law of Significance and Inspiration is a great law to focus on when you need motivation or when you feel that you have no purpose or you do not matter.

According to this law, your every contribution will affect the world. You were born with a gift, a mission and a purpose that only you can bring to the world with your uniqueness. Sharing your skills and gifts is really what you are here for.

We all have value to give. Our special gift is meant to be shared with the world and make a positive impact. So it does not matter how small and unusual our part in the world can be, it is important. But remember, to get something back, you need to put something in.

A person gets back what he puts into it. The true value of something directly results from the energy and intent invested in it. Each individual contribution is also a part of the whole. A small part also affects everyone. Therefore, giving in loving contributions gives life and inspiration to the whole.

For example, whenever you make a creative, loving contribution to the world around you, your actions encourage a similar positive behavior in others and that brings more positivity into your life.

You may not always feel important, but you are always important. Without your presence, the energy of the universe will transform drastically.

You may not always feel significant.
But you always are.

The twelfth Law of Karma is like The Law of Patience and Reward. It states you get what you deserve. This law means that the key to success lies in the energy and love you put into something.

The reward results from the energy
and love you have invested in
something.

Key takeaway – Contribute, no matter what happens.

CHANGING KARMA

Mindfulness transforms Karma: When you sit down and do not let your impulses turn into action.

Zen experts say daily meditation can turn bad Karma into good.

Karma means B happened because it relates to A in some way. There is a root cause of everything that happens. And each cause has its own effects, steps and side effects, at least at a non-quantum level. In short, when we talk about a person's Karma, we mean the sum of the direction of a person's life and the things that happen around that person. They can cause current situations, actions, thoughts, feelings, emotions and desires.

Most common mistake about Karma is to see it has having a fixed destiny. In actuality, it is the sum of trends that can lock us into a particular behavior pattern, which further creates a vicious circle of similar patterns. This way, we become prisoners of Karma.

But it is not necessary to be an inmate of Karma. We can always change our Karma. But there is that one moment that you ever have to change to break free from the vicious circle. Can you guess when that moment is?

Watch Your Impulses

This is how the mindfulness changes Karma. When you sit down, you do not allow your impulses to turn into actions. At that moment, you only see them. When you look at them, you immediately see that all those impulses in your mind come and go. They have a life of their own. They are not you, and you do not have to follow them. Not feeding or reacting to your impulses, you understand the nature of thoughts.

This process of mindfulness burns up the destructive impulses with the concentration, equanimity and non-doing. At the same time, creativity and creative impulses are no longer pressed by turbulent, destructive ones. Thus, mindfulness can reconnect the chain of actions and their associated results.

In doing so, we break our chains, free ourselves, and open up new directions for us to move in life. Without mindfulness, we can easily get carried away by the energy of the past, without realizing our own success and without a way out.

Our problem is always somewhere outside of us - be it the other person's fault, or the world's fault, so we are always looking to justify our own views and feelings. But by doing that, the present moment never becomes a new beginning, because we keep it from becoming one.

All Too Common

Karma, in one form or another, is found repeating in relationships, where the relationship dies or lacks something important from the start, which brings heartache, grief and bitterness. Eventually, we are likely to reap what we have sown. If you practice anger and isolation in a relationship for 40 years, you end up being imprisoned by anger and isolation. No big surprises. And given the role here, it's not satisfactory apportioning the blame here.

After all, it's our indifference that locks us in. We have become better at being out of touch with all of our possibilities, and have more and more stuck with our over-the-lifetime cultivated habits of not seeing, but only reacting and blaming.

If we want to change our Karma, we have to stop those things that cloud the mind and body, and color all our actions. It is not about doing good deeds. Instead, it means knowing who and what you are right now, that you are not your Karma. It means to align yourself with the way things actually are. It means to see things clearly.

Where to start?

Where do we start? Why not with our own mind? After all, it is the tool from which all of our thoughts and feelings arise. Impulses and perceptions from there lead to worldly actions. When we stop outward activity and practice being still, in the space, in the moment, we are deciding to break the flow of old Karma, and create a new, healthier Karma. It is the foundation of change, the transformation of the life we live.

The very act of stopping, of nurturing the moments of non-doing, of just watching, helps in putting us to an entirely different footing. How, you may ask? Because only by being in the moment we get a greater understanding, clarity and kindness that is less fearful or hurtful, and more honorable. Only what happens now happens later. If we don't have the mindfulness or the equanimity or the compassion now, how likely it is that it will magically appear later, when we are under stress or duress?

Conclusion

The 12 Laws of Karma can serve as guidelines or a roadmap to follow in daily life. These laws can help you understand how Karma actually works and how your thoughts and actions can affect you and the world around you.

Using Karma as a set of instructions in your life can make you be more mindful of your thoughts and actions before you make a decision.

Therefore, Karma is a lifestyle that fosters positive thinking and action.

Karma is not meant to be a punishment. It is present for the sake of education. How else is someone to learn how to be a good person if they are never taught that harmful action is wrong? A person only suffers if they have created the conditions for suffering.

Karma is not about doing good or doing bad.

You may hold spiritual beliefs and you may not. But understanding the Laws of Karma helps us to see the relationship between actions and consequences. There is a great freedom found in understanding how your actions work to change your life and the world around you.

Apply these laws to find a more fulfilled, productive, and impactful life.

List of 12 Laws of Karma

1. **The Law of Cause and Effect** - Your actions and thoughts have consequences.

2. **The Law of Creation** - You can only change your life by taking action.

3. **The Law of Humility** - You have to accept things in order to change them.

4. **The Law of Growth** - You need to change yourself before you can change your environment.

5. **The Law of Responsibility** - Take responsibility for the things that you have created, good and bad.

6. **The Law of Connection** - Past, present and future are connected closely.

7. **The Law of Focus** - Focus completely on the task at hand in order to accomplish it in the best possible way.

8. **The Law of Giving and Hospitality** - Your behavior should match your thoughts and actions.

9. **The Law of Here and Now** - You can't be present when you look back.

10. **The Law of Change** - The past repeats itself until you learn from it and take a new direction.

11. **The Law of Patience and Reward** - Long-term rewards require patience and constant work.

12. **The Law of Significance and Inspiration** - The reward results from the energy and love you have invested in something.

About Author

Manhardeep Singh is an India-based best-selling author, motivational speaker, and handwriting analyst. Gaining from the experience of one-on-one counseling sessions, Manhardeep pens down self-help books. His writings are focused on the topics of handwriting analysis and bringing the best out of life.

Manhardeep Singh has a Masters degree in Business Administration. He regularly writes articles in his blog www.manhardeep.com

Explore other books in the same series:

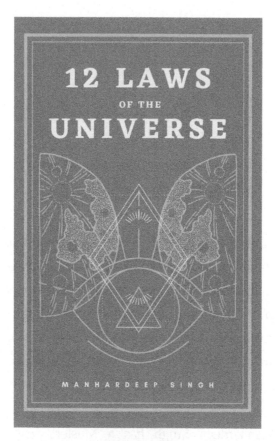

Also by the Author

STANDALONES:

DON'T FEAR THE MIC

MANHARDEEP SINGH

FROM THE AUTHOR OF 101 NUGGETS FOR LIFE

THE ULTIMATE BOOK OF MOTIVATION

MANHARDEEP SINGH

MANHARDEEP SINGH

THE STORY OF A WIMPY KID

ONE-LINERS SERIES:

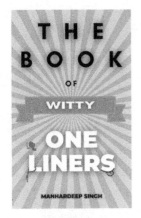

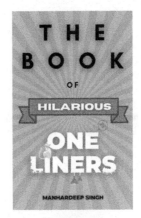

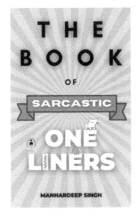

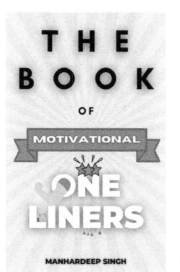

THE
BOOK
OF
MOTIVATIONAL
**ONE
LINERS**
MANHARDEEP SINGH

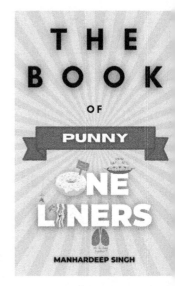

THE
BOOK
OF
PUNNY
**ONE
LINERS**
MANHARDEEP SINGH

DATING ESSENTIALS SERIES:

ARE YOU RELATIONSHIP READY?

DATING ESSENTIALS SERIES

KNOW IF YOU ARE READY FOR A SERIOUS RELATIONSHIP

MANHARDEEP SINGH

QUEEN BEE

DATING ESSENTIALS SERIES

THE ART OF ATTRACTING MEN

MANHARDEEP SINGH

LICENSED DATER

DATING ESSENTIALS SERIES

16 TYPES OF WOMEN AND WHAT THEY WANT

MANHARDEEP SINGH

HANDWRITING EXPERT SERIES:

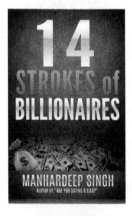

99 FOR SELF SERIES:

Made in the USA
Las Vegas, NV
18 December 2022